# The Muppet Guide to
# MAGNIFICENT
# MANNERS

*To Joanna and Adam Carver*

—J.H.

# The Muppet Guide to
# MAGNIFICENT MANNERS

Featuring Jim Henson's Muppets™

By James Howe

Illustrated by Peter Elwell

Muppet Press / Random House

Copyright © 1984 by Henson Associates, Inc. THE MUPPET SHOW, MUPPET, and MUPPET character names are trademarks of Henson Associates, Inc. All rights reserved under International and Pan-American Copyright Conventions. Published in the United States by Random House, Inc., New York, and simultaneously in Canada by Random House of Canada Limited, Toronto. A Muppet Press Book produced by Henson Organization Publishing in association with Random House, Inc.

*Library of Congress Cataloging in Publication Data:* Howe, James. The Muppet guide to magnificent manners. SUMMARY: The various Muppet characters illustrate the correct way to approach some common social situations. 1. Etiquette for children and youth. [1. Etiquette] I. Henson, Jim. II. Elwell, Peter, ill. III. Title.   BJ1857.C5H63   1984   395'.122 83-25063   ISBN: 0-394-86351-8 (trade); 0-394-96351-2 (lib. bdg.)
Manufactured in the United States of America   1   2   3   4   5   6   7   8   9   0

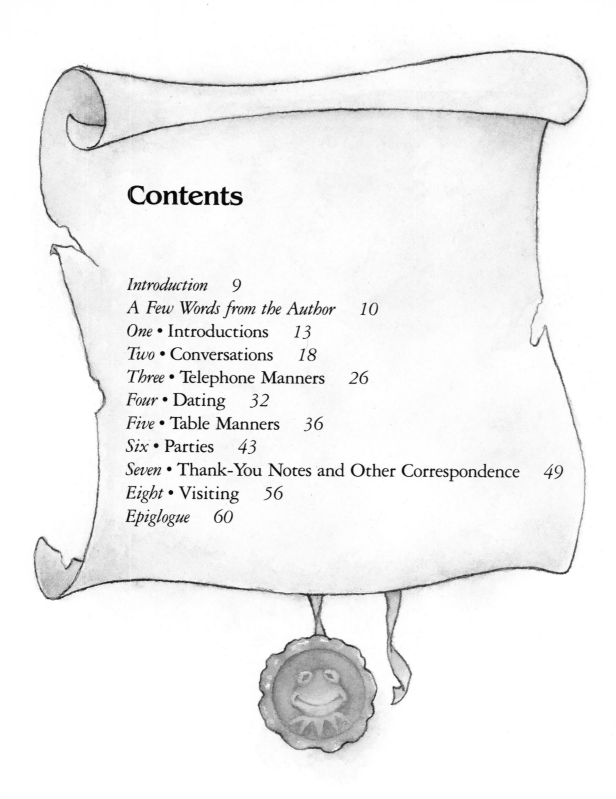

# Contents

# Introduction

How many times have you asked yourself: "Which present should I open first?" "What do I say after I've said hello?" "How do I tell someone his elbow is in my mashed potatoes?"

Not knowing what to do or say can be awkward and sometimes so embarrassant! At least, that's what they tell moi. Being the superstar that I am, I have been blessed with the remarkable ability to always do and say the right thing. I mean, who else knows just which fork to reach for when the vichyssoise is served? Or how to excuse oneself from the table at a restaurant just in time to avoid getting stuck with le bill?

Alas, some of my Muppet acquaintances (not the green kind, of course) are sorely ignorant of the fine points of proper behavior, as you will see from the sad stories told within these pages. I have tried (and tried and tried) to help them out. But did they listen? No. Of course, it is understandable that they did not. After all, when one is confronted with such a dazzling sight as moi, it is hard to keep the eyes and ears open at the same time.

So to give them the help they so desperately need, I have persuaded Kermy to sit down at his typewriteur and dash off this adorable little book. I would have written it moiself, but I have been très busy of late searching for just the right toothpaste to match my bathroom wallpaper.

Speaking of dashing off, I must. I hope you enjoy le book. Now when someone has his elbow in your mashed potatoes, you'll know exactly what to say ("Get your arm out of my spuds, bud, or you'll be looking through your lamb chop!"). This will be just one of the many times you'll be glad you read *The Muppet Guide to Magnificent Manners*.

# A Few Words from the Author

Thank you, Miss Piggy, for those . . . er . . . inspiring words.

    Actually, I'm glad Piggy asked me to write this book, because it gives me the opportunity to talk about something that matters a lot to me: good manners.

    Good manners are more than just do's and don'ts, you know. They're a way of getting along with others and making the world a more pleasant place in which to live. Here at the Muppet Theater I try to encourage the use of good manners at all times.

Sometimes I'm successful . . .

Sometimes I'm not . . .

    But successful or not, it's important to *try* to do the right thing. If you're not sure you know what the right thing is, please read on.

*Kermit the Frog*

# The Muppet Guide to
# MAGNIFICENT MANNERS

## *Chapter One*
# Introductions

Knowing how to introduce two or more people who have never met is something that will come in handy time and time again. With the help of a few simple rules, you'll be able to turn strangers into friends and silence into conversation and avoid situations such as the one Janice found herself in recently.

Ann Chovy, lead singer of the rock band Celestial Tuna, had just arrived to do a gig at the Muppet Theater. Janice, who's the lead singer with our band, the Electric Mayhem, had known Ann for years and was showing her around backstage when they bumped into Floyd Pepper, the bass player. No one said a word. Floyd stared at Ann. Ann stared at Floyd. Janice stared at the ceiling. Finally Floyd mumbled something and moved on. When Ann asked Janice why she hadn't introduced her, Janice said, "If two people are meant to groove on each other, their energy waves will just sort of flow out of their bods and, like, do a cosmic dance together. If the vibes are right, names don't matter, y'know?"

Well, names mattered to Ann Chovy. And they matter to most people. Instead of staring at the ceiling, what do you think Janice should have done?

1. Looked at Floyd and said, "Oh, Floyd, yer mustache needs trimming. Fer sher."
2. Turned to her friend and said, "Ann, this is that weird bass player I was telling you about."
3. Smiled and said, "Floyd, I'd like you to meet my old friend Ann Chovy."
4. Smiled and said, "Ann, I'd like you to meet our band's bass player, Floyd Pepper. Floyd, this is my old friend Ann Chovy."

Both 3 and 4 may seem like the right thing to do. But 4 is the correct answer. When you're introducing a man and a woman (or a boy and a girl), the woman's name comes first. For instance, if you had invited Gonzo over to your house, you would introduce Gonzo *to* your mother (if she hadn't fainted first) by saying "Mom, I'd like you to meet Gonzo." Then you might tell her a little something about him, like "He's been teaching me spoon hanging." And then you would reverse the introduction: "Gonzo, this is my mother, Mrs. Mustard." Always use the name the two people will use in talking to each other. Gonzo obviously isn't going to call your mother Mom, so "Mrs. Mustard" is the proper way to introduce her.

Here are three simple rules to help you in introducing one person to another:

1. Say the woman's name before the man's.
2. Say the older person's name before the younger person's ("Mr. Waldorf, this is my friend Scooter.").
3. Say the more important person's name before the less important person's.

That last one's an easy one to figure out if you're introducing the mayor and your cousin. But what if your father and your teacher are meeting for the first time? Even though your parents are important people, when you introduce them to other adults it's polite to say the other person's name first. For instance: "Mr. Stroganoff, this is my father." Or "Mr. Stroganoff, this is my father, Mr. Buckle." (Be sure to say your mother's or father's last name if it's different from yours.)

Here are some phrases that will help you in making introductions:

". . . I'd like you to meet . . ."

". . . this is . . ."

". . . may I introduce . . ."

". . . may I present . . ."

Or you can simply state the two names with perhaps an identifying phrase:

"Fred Finger, my new neighbor, Tommy Toes."

What if you're introducing yourself? It's probably easier than you think. Simply say hello, state your name, and tell a little something about yourself. For example: "Hello, I'm Scooter. I work with Kermit at the Muppet Theater."

And if you're being introduced to someone else? Simple again. Shake hands. Say "Hello" or "How do you do" or "I'm pleased to meet you." And before you know it, you'll be having a conversation with someone you didn't even know just a few minutes before.

Here are some helpful hints about introductions:

- Stand when you're being introduced.
- Shake hands. And don't be afraid to be the first one to put your hand forward.
- If a person has a title, use it. Say "How do you do, Dr. Cough-alot."

16

- If you forget the name of the person you're introducing, don't try to cover up. A lapse of memory can happen to anyone, and trying to pretend it isn't happening will only make it worse. Say something simple like "I'm sorry, but I've forgotten your name."
- If you don't catch the name of the person you're being introduced to, simply say "I'm sorry, I didn't hear your name."

One last word on introductions: Being introduced to your parents' friends and other adults can be confusing. Some adults like to be called by their first names, some by their titles (Mr., Mrs., Dr., etc.). Chances are they will let you know how they wish to be addressed. If you're not comfortable addressing them as they have requested, don't embarrass them by telling them so. Wait to discuss it with your parents later. When in doubt, use the person's title and last name.

Now that you've been introduced, you're ready to have a conversation. You're in luck, because that's our next chapter.

## Chapter Two
## Conversations

Gonzo once told me he thought that starting a conversation with someone he'd just met was as difficult as getting a mackerel to wear socks. But, as I told him, it *can* be done. If you pay close attention to other people—who they are and what they say—you'll be able to find the words you need to make a conversation happen.

Imagine you're at a party where you've just introduced yourself to Scooter. He now introduces himself to you much as he did in the last chapter.

"Hello, I'm Scooter," he says. "I work with Kermit at the Muppet Theater."

What might you say next to get a conversation going?

1. "Scooter—what a great name! Is it a nickname?"
2. "Working in a theater must be interesting. What kind of work do you do?"
3. "Why do you have to wear such thick glasses?"
4. "That's a neat jacket. I really like it."

All of the above are based on observations you made with either your eyes or your ears. And they are all good responses to Scooter—all except 3, that is. Answer 3 is a personal question that is none of your business. As such, it's out of place in any conversation.

So, a few suggestions to get a conversation going:

- Ask a question or make a comment based on something you've observed about the other person or something the other person has said.
- Give the person an honest compliment.
- Ask a general question ("Where do you go to school?" "Do you like horseback riding?").
- Make a simple statement about something you did recently or something you are going to do soon ("I saw the greatest movie yesterday." "I'm going white-water rafting this weekend.").

To keep the conversation going once it's started:

- Observe and listen to the other person.
- Ask questions.
- Look for common interests.
- Talk about what's going on around you ("This is a great party, isn't it?").
- Talk about yourself, your own interests and experiences—without bragging or hogging the conversation.

Speaking of hogging the conversation, when Miss Piggy and Link Hogthrob, one of the leading players of the Muppet Theater, were waiting for a bus recently, they had the following exchange:

19

Miss Piggy: Your performance in "Pigs in Space" was wonderful today, Link.

Link: As always, Piggy, my dear. As always.

Miss Piggy: Well, what I meant was—

Link: You were overwhelmed. I understand. So was I.

Miss Piggy: No, actually, I—

Link: Drat! It looks like it's going to rain.

Miss Piggy: Well, I'm sure the bus will be here soon.

Link: You're crazy. This bus is always late.

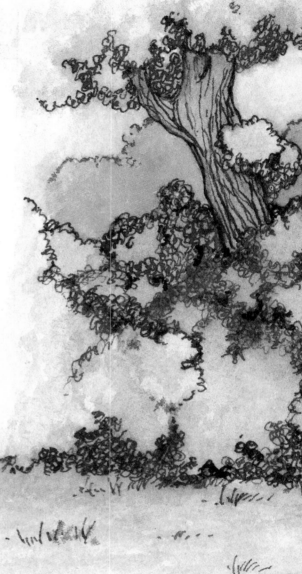

The arrival of the bus four seconds later brought an abrupt end to the conversation, but not before Link had broken quite a few rules of good behavior. Which of the following did he mess up on?

1. Try not to interrupt. If you must, say "Excuse me for interrupting, but . . ."
2. Don't brag or exaggerate.
3. Don't pretend to know more than you do.
4. When someone compliments you, say "Thank you." Don't belittle the other person ("What, this old thing?") or get a swelled head ("Yeah, I know I'm great.").
5. Don't finish other people's sentences for them.
6. If you give an opinion, state it as such, not as fact. If you disagree with someone else's opinion, don't say "You're wrong" or "You're crazy." Say something like "Do you think so? Gee, I don't see it like that. I think . . ."

The only one Link missed was 3, and that's probably because the bus came before he could get to it.

When it's time for a conversation to end, end it simply and directly by letting the other person know you've got to stop talking now. You might say something like:

"Well, I have to go now. It's been nice talking with you."

"There's my dad. I've got to run. See you tomorrow."

"I've really had a good time. Hope I'll see you again soon."

And then say "Good-bye."

Whatever you do, don't end your conversation the way Link did when the bus came to his stop: "Well, Piggy, I have to go now. Words cannot express how much you've enjoyed the pleasure of my company."

Link was right. Words couldn't. Miss Piggy hit him with her pocketbook instead.

# Kermit's Do Words and Don't Words

There are certain words that oil the wheels of good conversation and keep it running along smoothly. Little words like *please, thank you, may I, you're welcome, excuse me,* and *I'm sorry.* Here are some examples of how to use them.

| DO SAY | DON'T SAY | WHEN |
|---|---|---|
| "Please" | "Gimme that." "Pass the salt." "Keep the noise down." "Lemme do it." | you want something |
| "Thank you" | "Ooo, this is the ugliest tie I ever saw." "I already have a nose comb." "Mmph." | you receive something—a gift, a compliment, a loan, a favor, service in a restaurant or store, or when someone does something for you |
| "You're welcome" | "Huh? Oh, sure." | someone says "Thank you" |
| "May I . . ."* | "Can I . . ."* "Let me . . ." | you want permission to do something |
| "Excuse me" | "Boy, am I beat!" | you yawn |

24

| | | |
|---|---|---|
| "Excuse me" | "Comin' through!" | you move through a crowd |
| "Excuse me" | "Watch it!" | you cut or pass in front of someone |
| "Excuse me" | "Hey!" | you must interrupt |
| "Excuse me?" "I beg your pardon" | "Huh?" | you don't understand something someone has said |
| "I'm sorry" | (shrug and look the other way) | you're late, you bump into someone, you break or spill something |

*"May I . . ." is used to ask permission. "Can I . . ." asks if you are able. You would ask "May I leave the table?" if you wished to be excused. You would ask "Can I leave the table?" if your brother had put glue on your chair and there was serious question about your ability to get up.

## Chapter Three
# Telephone Manners

One night after almost everyone had gone home, the telephone rang backstage at the Muppet Theater. My assistant, Scooter, who was putting away the props, went to answer it.

"Yeah?" he said, popping his gum loudly into the receiver.

"Who is this?" the voice on the other end asked.

"Who is *this?*" was Scooter's reply.

"I asked you first," said the caller.

"Well, I'm not telling until you tell," Scooter said.

There followed a long silence, during which both Scooter and the caller fumed. Each felt that the other had behaved badly. Who do you think was guilty of poor manners?

1. Scooter.
2. The caller.

You're right if you picked 1. But you're also right if you picked 2. Neither Scooter nor the caller handled the situation properly. And their failure to observe a few simple telephone courtesies led to hurt feelings and a breakdown of communication.

## Receiving a Telephone Call

"Hello" is the correct way to answer the phone—not "Yeah?" and not "Who is this?" If the call is for you, identify yourself: "This is Scooter speaking." Or "Hi, Gonzo. This is Scooter." Don't say "This is me" or "You got 'im" or "What d'ya want?" If the caller doesn't identify himself, ask "Who is this?"

If the call is for someone else and that person is in, don't hold the phone two inches from your mouth and scream "Mom! It's for you!" In fact, don't scream at all. Say "Just a moment, please. I'll get her." Then put the phone down gently, go find the other person, and tell her she's wanted on the phone.

Again, if the caller hasn't given you his name, you should ask "Who is this, please?" or "Who's calling, please?" or "May I tell her who's calling?"

If the call is for someone who is home but can't come to the phone, you don't have to say where the person is (as in "My sister's in the bathroom. And knowing her, she'll be in there for the next three hours."). Just say "She's in, but she can't come to the phone right now. May I take a message?" Or if the call is for someone who isn't home, say "He isn't in right now. May I take a message?"

*Always* offer to take a message and *always* write the message down. If necessary, say "Excuse me while I get a pencil and paper." When taking the message, be sure it's clear to you. Ask the caller to repeat himself if you need him to, ask for the spelling if you don't understand a name, and read back all telephone numbers to make sure you've gotten them right.

## Making a Telephone Call

When you make a telephone call, you have an advantage over the person on the other end. After all, you probably have a pretty good idea whom you're calling. But the person answering the phone has no idea who you are, until you say so. Don't turn your advantage into an opportunity to play "Guess Who?" Instead, let the other person know right away who you are.

If you recognize the voice on the other end as the person you're calling, say "Hello, Scooter. This is Gonzo." Or, if not, say hello, identify yourself, and ask for the person to whom you wish to speak: "Hello, this is Gonzo the Great. May I speak to Kermit, please?"

Suppose the person you're calling isn't in. What might you say next?

1. "Well, where is he?"
2. "May I leave a message, please?"
3. "What's he doing?"
4. "Oh, great. Now what am I supposed to do?"

If you've resisted the temptation to play detective and you've figured out that what you're supposed to do is not the other person's problem, you've undoubtedly come to the correct conclusion that you should ask to leave a message. Make your message short and to the point—something along the lines of "Would you please ask Kermit to call me when he gets in?" Or "Please tell him I'll call again after supper."

When you're making a telephone call:
- Be considerate—keep your calls short.
- Ask "Is this a good time for you to talk?" or "Do you have a few minutes?" if you want to talk for a while. Don't take other people's time for granted.
- Don't call early in the morning, late at night, or at dinnertime.
- Speak in a clear voice. Don't shout, mumble, or whisper.
- Let the phone ring at least six times before hanging up.
- If you reach an answering machine, don't hang up. Leave a clear, short message.

## Wrong Numbers

It turned out that the phone call we were talking about at the beginning of this chapter wasn't for Scooter anyway. The caller was trying to reach Luigi's International House of Toast. It seems he dialed a wrong number.

If *you* reach what seems to be a wrong number, simply ask "Is this

555-3419?" (or whatever number you dialed). If the other person says "No, it isn't," say "I'm sorry to have bothered you. I have a wrong number."

If you receive a call that's a wrong number, say "I'm sorry, but you have the wrong number." There's no need to get into a long conversation or answer personal questions.

## Saying Good-bye

Ending a telephone conversation can be tricky if the other person doesn't want to get off and you do. Say something like: "Well, it's been great talking to you. I have to get off now. I've got homework to do." Or "I've got to say good-bye now. Someone else wants to use the phone."

Don't slam the phone down, as Scooter did—especially if your thumb is in the way!

## Chapter Four
# Dating

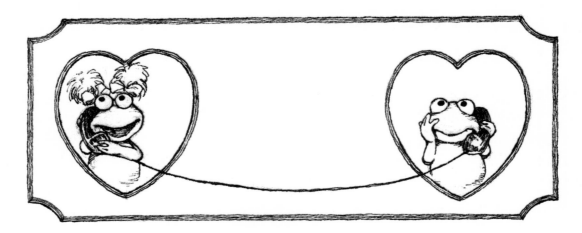

One reason you might be using the telephone—either now or when you're a little older—is to ask someone out on a date. At one time it was considered proper only for boys to ask girls out. Now it's okay for girls to ask boys as well. But whether you're a boy or a girl, getting up the nerve to ask someone out—and then actually *doing* it—isn't always easy, especially the first time.

Just ask my nephew Robin.

One day a new girl showed up at his school. Her name was Ida Claire. Robin fell head-over-flippers in love. He wanted to ask her out in the worst way. And that's exactly what he did.

Over and over he practiced what he was going to say. When he could put it off no longer, he picked up the phone and called her.

"Hello, Ida. This is Robin," he said. "Um . . . er . . . I was . . . uh . . . wondering if you were busy this Saturday afternoon."

"Yes, I am," Ida replied. "Why?"

"Oh, no reason," said Robin hastily. "Well, I've got to go now. Good-bye." And he hung up.

Ida thought Robin was a little strange, and Robin wondered if he'd ever dare ask Ida—or anyone—out again. Maybe it was the way he asked her. How do you think Robin should have asked Ida for a date?

1. "So, Ida, what are you doing this Saturday afternoon?"
2. "Would you like to go out with me, Ida?"
3. "Would you like to go with me to the movies this Saturday afternoon?"
4. "If you don't go out with me, Ida, I'll move back to the swamp."

Well, besides the fact that Robin doesn't have the bus fare to the swamp, threats will get him nowhere. No, the correct way to ask for a date is 3. The simple and direct approach is best. Tell the other person what you have planned (a movie, a party, skating), and when, and then ask if he or she would like to join you. It's a good idea to have another plan in mind in case the person says no. For instance:

"I've got two tickets to the hockey game Friday. Would you like to join me?"

"I'd love to, but I have plans Friday night."

"Well, how about going with me to a movie Saturday afternoon then?"

"Okay, that would be fun."

Great, you've got a date! Now, there are several things that should be made clear before you actually go out:

- Where you're going.
- Who's paying. Let the other person know if you're intending to

pay ("It will be my treat" or "I'd like to pay for the tickets") or if each person is expected to pay his or her own way ("We'll go Dutch treat, okay?"). Any arrangement is all right—as long as it's made clear up front and both people have agreed to it.

- How you're getting to and from where you're going.
- What time you'll pick the other person up (the person *asking* usually picks the other person up at his or her home) and what time you expect you'll be back. (Traditionally, the boy takes the girl home. However, it doesn't really matter who takes whom home unless it's after dark. Then, for safety's sake, the boy should see the girl home.)
- Who will be with you, if anyone.
- If special clothes are needed. (For instance, if you're going on a picnic which will include swimming, you want to be sure to let the other person know to bring a suit.)

Once he learned the proper way to ask, Robin called Ida back and asked her to go with him to a school dance. This time, she said yes.

Robin was so happy, he was hopping on air for days. But soon he began to worry. His mind was filled with questions about what it was like to go on a date. And so he did what he always does when in doubt. He came to talk to me. Now, I won't say I always have *all* the answers, but when Robin's worried about something, I do my best to help him out. Here's some of what we talked about:

34

"What do I do when I pick Ida up at her house, Uncle Kermit?"

"Well, first of all, Robin, try not to be late. Then, when you arrive, be sure to introduce yourself to Ida's parents and tell them where you're going and when you'll be back. After you've talked for a few minutes, say good-bye to them—and then you're on your way."

"What do I do at the dance if I want to spend time with my other friends?"

"You and Ida can spend time with your friends together. Introduce her to people she doesn't know but don't wander away from her. She's your date and you should stick together."

"What if I'm having such a good time I don't want to leave when I said I would?"

"Take your date home at the agreed-upon time."

"What if we stop for ice cream and I don't have enough money?"

"Well, Robin, try to avoid that situation by taking extra money with you—even if you're going Dutch treat. And before you order the ice cream, check to make sure you have enough money to pay for it."

"Gee, Uncle Kermit, when I think about taking Ida out on a date, my stomach gets all jumpy."

"Don't worry, Robin. You're just nervous. But it will pass quickly. And soon you'll be having such a good time, you'll forget all about it."

"Phew, that's good to hear. Thanks, Uncle Kermit."

"You're welcome, Robin. Have fun!"

"I'll try, Uncle Kermit. I'll try."

35

## Chapter Five
# Table Manners

### What Is Wrong with This Picture?

1. Gonzo is using his soup spoon when he should be using his dessert spoon.
2. Spaghetti should never be eaten with the hands. Rather, one should drop one's head directly into the plate and inhale.
3. A knife should not be used to fling peas. A fork is the proper utensil.
4. Creamed spinach is never worn with plaid.
5. JUST ABOUT EVERYTHING IS WRONG WITH THIS PICTURE!!

You got it—the correct answer is 5.

## The Table

Setting the table and being sure of which dish or utensil to use at what time can be confusing until you've learned the basics.

Let's start with silverware. Most often you'll be dealing with just three pieces: the knife, the fork, and the spoon. The fork is placed directly to the left of the plate, the knife directly to the right (with its cutting edge facing the plate), and the spoon directly to the right of the knife. Sometimes there may be additional pieces: the salad fork, for instance, and the soup spoon. The salad fork is placed to the left of the regular fork, the soup spoon to the right of the regular spoon.

A good rule to remember when in doubt about which piece of silverware to use: The utensil *farthest away* from the plate is used *first*. Since soup and salad are eaten before the main course, you would know to eat them with the spoon and fork farthest away from the plate.

The bread-and-butter plate, with the butter knife lying across it, and the salad plate are placed at the top and to the left of the main dish respectively. To the top right is the glass. And finally to the left of the entire setting is the folded napkin.

Some words of advice on using the above dishes and utensils:
- Use your butter knife to take the amount of butter you want, then put it on your bread-and-butter plate. Break off a piece of bread and butter it from the butter on your plate. Don't butter the whole piece of bread at one time.
- When helping yourself to food, use the serving utensils provided—not your own silverware.
- Don't push your food with your fingers. Use your knife or a piece of bread.
- Once you've used a utensil during the meal, don't lay it back

down on the table. When not using your knife or fork, rest them diagonally across the top of your plate. When you've finished eating, lay your knife and fork across the plate side-by-side.

- When eating soup, dip the spoon away from you—not toward you. Bring the spoon up to your mouth (it may take a little practice to do this without spilling). Don't blow on the soup or slurp it. Gently draw the soup in from the side of the spoon—don't put the whole spoon into your mouth.

- The napkin is placed across the lap, never tucked into the shirt or the pants. Always wipe your mouth with your napkin before drinking so you don't leave food on the rim of your glass. When eating food with your hands, don't lick your fingers—use your napkin. One thing you should never use your napkin for is a handkerchief.

- At the end of the meal, place your napkin loosely on the table to the left of your plate.

## Dinner Is Served

Dinner is commonly served in one of three ways:

**Buffet style.** All the food is put out in large serving dishes on one main table, along with plates, napkins, and silverware. Each person helps himself and then eats at another table.

**Waiter or maid service.** In restaurants or in homes with hired help, dinner will be served to you. In a restaurant, the meal that you order will be placed before you. In someone's home, the maid will bring each dish to you and you will help yourself.

**Family style.** Food is placed in serving dishes on the table and each dish is passed so that every person can help himself.

Speaking of passing food: If what you want is within your arm's length *and you don't have to reach across someone else's plate for it,* you may reach rather than ask for it to be passed. You should not reach across the table, however. Instead, ask the person closest to what you want to pass it. If someone else asks for food to be passed, pass the whole dish— not one roll or a spoonful of potatoes.

What do you do if you don't like the food being served? If you're in your own home, that's for your parents to decide. If you're in someone else's home, you should always help yourself to the main dish—whether you like it or not. Other food, however, you may politely refuse. Don't make a big deal about it—just say "No, thank you" and pass the dish.

In general, if you're a guest and you don't know what to do, watch to see what your host and hostess do. Then follow their example.


## Some Do's and Don'ts

- DO sit up straight.
- DON'T tilt your chair back.

40

- DO bring the food up to your mouth, not your mouth down to your plate.
- DON'T talk with food in your mouth.
- DO wait to start eating until your parents or your host or hostess begins.
- DON'T comb your hair or otherwise groom yourself at the table.
- DO chew with your mouth closed.
- DON'T announce "I'm through!" or "I'm stuffed!" when you're finished eating.
- DO compliment the cook on the meal.

## What to Do When . . .

**You spill something.** Use your knife or spoon to scoop it up. For stains, wet your napkin with some water and dab at it. Say "I'm sorry." If it's a large spill, offer to help your host or hostess clean it up.

**The food is too hot to eat.** Just leave it until it's cooled down. Don't blow on it. If you've already eaten something hot and it's burning the inside of your mouth, reach for your water and drink . . . fast!

**You have to cough or burp.** Turn your head to the side and cover your mouth or nose with a napkin.

**You must remove something from your mouth.** Try to roll it with your tongue onto your fork or spoon. Don't take it out with your hands. If something's caught between your teeth, wait until the meal has ended. Then ask to be excused and go to the bathroom to deal with it. If it's really bothering you, don't wait for the meal to end. Excuse yourself and go to the bathroom.

**You must leave the table.** Say "Excuse me" and leave. You don't have to say where you're going.

## At a Restaurant

The same good table manners you'd use in your own or someone else's home should be brought with you to a restaurant. A few new rules apply, however:

- If you need the waiter, don't shout for him or snap your fingers. Call out in a soft voice "Waiter" or "Excuse me" and raise your hand slightly.
- If you drop your napkin or silverware, ask the waiter for a replacement.
- If you spill your drink, ask the waiter to please clean it up and get you another one.
- If you don't understand something on the menu, ask the waiter to explain it. Even adults ask for explanations.
- If you get the wrong food or it's not served the way you ordered it, you may return it. Say something like "I asked for this hamburger to be cooked rare, and it's well-done. Would you please take this back and bring me another?"
- As you can see, the waiter works hard to please you. You should always leave a tip to let him know you appreciated his service. The general rule for tipping is to leave 15 percent of the total amount of the bill. If the bill comes to ten dollars, for instance, you would leave a dollar and a half.

## Chapter Six
## Parties

I never thought I'd see the day Bunsen Honeydew would give a party. You know Bunsen—he's the one in the white coat who's so busy inventing things he never leaves his laboratory.

Well, a while back he came up with what he considered his greatest invention yet—talking shoes. ("It was simple really," he said. "Everyone's known for years that shoes have tongues. It was just a matter of getting them to work.") When he mentioned it to Fozzie, Fozzie suggested that he have a party to celebrate.

"Great idea!" said Bunsen. "Tell everybody to come over about seven."

When we arrived, Bunsen was in the middle of teaching his shoes the Gettysburg Address.

"Come in, come in!" he cried.

We did. And then we stood around for about an hour while Bunsen and his shoes debated whether or not sneakers could talk faster than loafers.

Getting bored with nibbling on nothing but our own fingernails, we left.

Where did Bunsen go wrong?
He didn't realize that a successful party needs:

1. A band with a good clam player.
2. A chicken juggler.
3. Planning.
4. A laugh track.

Well, while Gonzo might think the answer is 2,
the correct answer is 3.

It's important to plan your party carefully. Probably you and your parents will plan your party together. Here are some questions you'll want to ask in order to avoid the kind of disaster that befell Bunsen:

- What kind of party do I want? (birthday, surprise, barbecue, picnic, costume)
- Where will the party be held? (basement, living room, backyard, park)
- How many people shall I invite? (Where you're having the party may affect the number of people you can ask.)
- Whom shall I invite? (Make a list.)
- When will the party be held? (weekend, evening, day, holiday)
- What kinds of refreshments shall I serve my guests?
- Will I have any special entertainment? (Whether it's games, dancing, or movies, plan activities that you think your guests would enjoy, not just what *you* would most enjoy doing.)
- How will I decorate? (streamers, balloons, handmade decorations)

You should invite your guests one and a half to two weeks before the party, either in person, by telephone, or by written invitation. Written invitations—printed ones, the kind where you fill in the blanks, or ones you make yourself—are best because everything is written down and less likely to be forgotten.

Invitations should include:

- Your name.
- Date and time of the party.
- Place of the party.
- Anything special the guest needs to know (Come in a costume. Wear old clothes. This is a surprise party—don't tell Fozzie!).

- Response instructions. If you put R.S.V.P.* on your invitation, be sure to include your phone number.

Greet your guests at the door. Take their coats or show them where to put them. Point out where the refreshments are.

If it's your birthday, your guests will probably hand you a gift at the door. If they do, say thank you and put it with your others. If they don't hand you a gift, don't say "Where's my present?" They may have forgotten it, they may not have known it was your birthday, or they may not have been able to afford a gift. In any event, your pointing it out to them won't magically produce the missing gift—it will only embarrass them. Don't do it.

If your guests don't know other people or they're shy, introduce them to one another.

If you play games, remember that the object isn't to win but to entertain your guests. It's okay to keep the first prize you win. But if you win more than once, give the prizes to the runners-up. And if you lose, be a good sport about it.

When it comes time to open your presents, put them all in one area and open them in random order. Don't favor one person's gift over another, either by opening it first or by praising it more than the others. Respond to each gift with an enthusiastic remark and a thank you ("Wow, an electric banana peeler! I've always wanted one. Thanks!"). Don't say "I have a calculator already" or "I hate model airplanes."

When your guests leave, see them to the door. Say good-bye and thank them again for their gifts.

---

*Miss Piggy says that R.S.V.P. stands for the French *répondez s'il vous plâit,* or "Let me know if you're planning to show up!" Literally: "Please reply."

And when the party's over, don't immediately grab all your presents and head for your room. Your parents worked hard to make your party a success. Pitch in and help them clean up.

When you receive a party invitation, respond right away. Say "Yes, I'd love to come," or "No, I'm sorry, I can't make it." Don't ask "Who else is coming?" or "What are you going to have to eat?"

If it's a birthday party, be sure to bring a gift. If you can't afford it, bring something inexpensive or make something yourself.

When you arrive at the party, say hello to your host and his parents. If it's his birthday, say "Happy birthday" and give him his gift.

If your host doesn't introduce you to people you don't know, introduce yourself.

Whenever food is served, games are played, or presents are opened, go along with it without complaining, even if you're not happy about it. If you wish things were done differently, do them differently—at your *own* party.

Don't play rough indoors—you might break or damage something. If you do break or spill something, say you're sorry and offer to help clean it up.

And when it's time to leave, be sure to say good-bye to your host and his parents—and tell them you had a wonderful time!

## Chapter Seven
# Thank-You Notes and Other Correspondence

Some people will use any excuse they can think of *not* to send a thank-you note.

Unfortunately, there really is *no* good excuse for not sending a thank-you note. Thank-you notes—after you've received a gift or a special favor, after you've been a guest in someone's home, or after you've been a guest at a party—let the other person know how much you appreciate their thoughtfulness and all the trouble they may have gone to on your behalf. And even if you've already thanked them in person, they'll be glad to get a note from you.

Thank-you notes should always be sent promptly and should be handwritten. Even if you use a printed card, add a few lines of your own to make it personal.

All right. You've gotten out your best pen, your nicest paper, you've turned off the TV, and you're ready to write! Now *what* do you say?

If you're like Sam the Eagle, the Muppet guardian of good taste, you'll have an easier time with the gifts you really like than with those you don't. After his birthday party recently, Sam sat down to write his thank-yous. His first note was to Fozzie, and since he liked what Fozzie had given him, he had no problem finding just what he wanted to say:

Dear Fozzie,

Thank you so much for the coffee maker. I've needed one for a long time. To think it will not only perk my coffee but play the National Anthem - my favorite song - at the same time! I just can't think of a better way to start the day.

It was really thoughtful of you.

Yours sincerely,
SAM the Eagle

But when it came to Floyd Pepper's gift, Sam didn't know what to say. He thought and he thought. And then he wrote:

Dear Floyd,

I have read the book you gave me – <u>101 Ways to Be Cool</u>. There must be some mistake. I can find no references to air conditioners or even ice cubes. What I do find is sick, disgusting, and distasteful. I hope you will have the good sense not to give me such a gift in the future.

Sincerely,
SAM the Eagle

Sam needn't have worried. After a note like that, he's not likely to get *any* gifts from Floyd in the future.

You shouldn't lie when you're thanking someone for a gift you don't like ("I *love* the sweater!"). Neither should you say everything you feel, as Sam did. Just find a nice way to express your appreciation for the thoughtfulness of the giver—and if you can find *anything* nice to say about the gift, say it.

If you're thanking someone for entertaining you as a house or party guest, you might say something like:

"I had a great time at your party. The games were a lot of fun and the cake was delicious. Thanks for inviting me."

"Thank you for having me as your guest last weekend. You really made me feel at home. I enjoyed the picnic on Saturday and that trip to the falls was terrific. I can't wait to get my pictures developed."

There are other reasons to write people besides to say thank you. If you have friends or relatives who live far away, writing is a good and inexpensive way to keep in touch. Or when you're away from home—at camp, traveling, or on vacation—postcards or letters to your family and friends will let them know how you're doing—and give you a chance to share the fun you're having. And, of course, when someone is sick or has a birthday, they'll really appreciate being remembered. If you send a card at such times, don't forget to write a few lines of your own.

## Chapter Eight
# Visiting

When you're a guest in someone's home, you'll have a great opportunity to put into practice all the magnificent manners you've learned. Whether you're staying overnight or spending the weekend (or even longer), your visit will be more enjoyable for everyone if you are a thoughtful and considerate guest. And there's a better chance you'll be invited back!

Fozzie had really been looking forward to Gonzo's spending the weekend with him, but by Saturday morning he couldn't wait for Gonzo to leave. And no wonder! Gonzo juggled Fozzie's priceless porcelain banana collection, put his ice cream down on the radiator, and spent two hours on the phone with his girlfriend, Camilla—who happened to be visiting her sister in another state!

Gonzo made a lot of mistakes. Here are some suggestions that would have helped make his visit with Fozzie a more pleasant one. Keep them in mind the next time *you're* a houseguest.

- Fit in with the routine of the people you're staying with. Don't try to make them do things your way or say, "But this isn't how we do it at *our* house."

- Be on time for meals.
- Don't complain—about *anything*.
- Be helpful. Make your own bed. Pick up your clothes—and keep them in whatever place you've been given. Offer to help with such household chores as setting the table and washing the dishes.
- Use the towels set out for you. If you don't know which are yours, ask.
- Clean up after yourself in the bathroom.

- If you're hungry, ask if you may have a snack. Don't go into the refrigerator unless you've been given permission to.
- Don't snoop around in other people's belongings.
- If you have special needs, tell your hosts soon after you arrive ("I'd like to go to church on Sunday." "I have to take this medicine with milk three times a day.").
- If you want to borrow something, ask first, treat it with care, and return it before you leave.
- Don't use the telephone without asking. If you do use it, don't stay on for a long time. And if you call home, call collect.
- If you break or spill something, say you're sorry and help clean it up.
- Treat everything in your hosts' home with care and respect.

- Let your hosts know you appreciate what they're doing for you.
- Don't juggle—with *anything!*
- When it's time to leave, check to be sure you have all your belongings. And don't forget to thank everyone and to say good-bye to everyone.
- Within a few days of your return home, write a thank-you note.

One thing Gonzo *did* do right was to bring his host a small gift of appreciation. It wasn't his fault that Fozzie didn't care for chocolate-covered tires. Whatever it is, it's always nice to bring your host—or his parents—something as a way of thanking them for having you in their home. A box of candy, a basket of fruit, or a plant is always a welcome gift. Or you can send something after you've returned home.

Being a host can be fun too. After all, most people like to share who they are and what they like to do with other people. But be sensitive to your guest. Just because you enjoy playing with your sticker collection doesn't mean your guest is going to. Offer a choice of activities ("We could play in my room, go roller-skating, or go down to the pond—what would you like to do?"). And if he or she seems bored with what you're doing, suggest that you switch to something else. But don't feel you have to entertain a guest every single minute. Quiet time—time for reading, writing letters, or watching TV—is okay too.

Whether you're a guest or a host, the key to a good visit is consideration for other people.

But after all, that's what good manners are all about!

# Epiglogue

Ah, I see you have finished the book. What perfect timing! I have just this moment returned from my whirlwind tour of les drugstores. (You have no idea how hard it is to find a toothpaste in mauve!)

So—now you know the right fork from the left. Quel relief to think that you no longer run the risk of embarrassing your family, your friends, and Western civilization. I'm so-o-o glad this little book of Kermy's and mine was of such help. Yes, yes, I know Kermy actually wrote the thing, but where would he have been without moi's inspiration, hmm?

Good luck! And if you don't remember every little thing you've read here, just ask yourself: What would Miss Piggy do?*

Kissy kissy,

*And do the opposite! KERMIT

**About the Author** James Howe has been minding his manners ever since his mother told him, "Jimmy, Jimmy, strong and able,/Get your elbows off the table."

He has written many books for children, including *Bunnicula, Howliday Inn, The Celery Stalks at Midnight, Morgan's Zoo, The Hospital Book,* and *The Case of the Missing Mother* (another Muppet Press book, featuring his personal favorite—Animal).

Mr. Howe lives in New York City.

**About the Illustrator** Peter Elwell is a young artist whose work has appeared in many magazines, including *The National Lampoon* and *Muppet Magazine.* His children's books include *The King of the Pipers,* which he also wrote, and *Ten Years Beyond Baker Street.*

Mr. Elwell lives in New York City.